Inflorescence:

The Pasture at Rest

poems by

Marjorie Gowdy

Finishing Line Press
Georgetown, Kentucky

Inflorescence:

The Pasture at Rest

Copyright © 2023 by Marjorie Gowdy
ISBN 979-8-88838-185-4 First Edition
All rights reserved under International and Pan-American Copyright Conventions. No part of this book may be reproduced in any manner whatsoever without written permission from the publisher, except in the case of brief quotations embodied in critical articles and reviews.

ACKNOWLEDGMENTS

"The Ivy Tree" was published in the 2018 edition of *Artemis Journal*.
"Organelle" is published in the Fall 2021 edition of *Floyd County Moonshine*.
"Last of the Blue Azures" was exhibited as a poem on display at the Lynchburg, VA, River Walk in Spring 2021.
"Hirundo" was published in the 2022 edition of *Artemis Journal*.

Publisher: Leah Huete de Maines
Editor: Christen Kincaid
Cover Art: Marjorie Gowdy
Author Photo: Marjorie Gowdy
Cover Design: Elizabeth Maines McCleavy

Order online: www.finishinglinepress.com
also available on amazon.com

Author inquiries and mail orders:
Finishing Line Press
PO Box 1626
Georgetown, Kentucky 40324
USA

Table of Contents

Inflorescence 1

Resting in Tithonia 2

Hirundo 3

American Bittersweet 4

Savior 5

The Furies 6

Heart of Sunflower 7

A Murmuration 8

The Great Dispersal 9

Ravens in the Wood 10

Rufous Flies 11

Last of the Blue Azures 12

Summer Spring 13

The Ivy Tree 14

Leave-Taking 15

Organelle 16

Papilio 17

The Talisman 18

Fibonacci's Flowers 19

For my love James Hartley and my treasures:
Finley Hartley and Michael, Jessica, Ava, and Ivan Conway Hartley.
All of this is because of you.

Inflorescence

Dry winds dregs of summer push over hardened stalks
Playful petals tickle umber disc florets
Rudbeckia hirta hashes out shortening days.

I deadhead. A role at equinox for the hunched gardener
Once lissome once careless of the flowers
Whose Latin names my father taught my mother.

Now, sun southward, I amble among the chest-high Susans
Pluck off worn receptacles, toss to cool currents
Tuck hirta in my curls.

Sacrament of the stamen sacrificed to winter's dirt
Brother lost to autumn's embers
Flowers return. He cannot.

Resting in Tithonia

Genus *Bombus*
Two-score days to get it right

Prepare to fall, alighting the defiant Fibonaccis
Ovaries ungoverned

Sleep after solstice, petals curled into black fur.

Hirundo

Our sun is midway through the northern sky.
Frost teases wild roses winding along lines of an aching fence.
A waking blue sweat bee seeks tattered pollen larders from the fall.
Violet-bright blooms inch along the redbud's branch.

An anxious time.
Flattened timothy, quartz luminous in the half-frozen creek.
Misted lens on early morning trysts of the cardinal, the bluebird, the wren.
We can yet see straight down the valley of poplars to an empty road.

They give us four months, the passerines.
A scout arrives first, blustery after its vernal journey.
I'm feeding the horses, surrounded suddenly in blur of orange and blue.
Fearless straw thieves, they burrow and squawk.

I wait for them, their altricial promise in song.
They swoop diffidently, differently than the mocker,
more "hey" than "get out."
Didactics for weeks as downy young fly from stable to high wire.

Then, as they finish off gnats and green horse flies,
a final sitting. Blistering tar, gravel, and rest. Swallows disappeared in dry heat.
Passed by. Passed on. I could jump to catch them as they leave.
But it is *Hirundo's* burden to keep the barn raised.

American Bittersweet

Celastrus scandens. American bittersweet
false bittersweet
borne along hills, mountains, valleys, this red clay land,
by bluebirds to narrow valleys where the Tutelo lived.

Indigenous bittersweet
not the thorn'd invader
bark's meat a confection
berries' bane for the uninitiated.

These new men breathe fire
fling weapons guns anger on our back roads now.
Arrogant as the jay, they bleed sharpened ire into streams
booted prints in foul mud.

In our comfortable gated houses vines slashed
grass scoured
columns of false stone
Do they live here?

Poison slips into veins as sluice into a stream
as the maid passes a tankard
as taints twist into braided rancor
as ink stained with revulsion seeps into men's spleens.

How to tell the story of first columns
bronzed ambitious men who cut wood
ate bounty, stalked game, chased the brave Tutelo
from a berth in the bittersweet.

Fruit sweet in spring, greens in a low valley mist
yellow at midsummer, burns at autumn, seared.
Caustic mordant crimson tempts the wrath of ancients.
Bird blue flees with her last red berry. A poplar crashes, alone.

Savior

In the stooped squat of age, I grab a plastic cup and lid
        stealthily bend toward the corner
        where he cowers.

Sometimes she with eight legs and a thousand babes
        often a skeeter-killer or trembling moth
        swept up in darkness thrown softly to waiting leaves.

If they sting or bite I kill them dead
        on the spot with bodily force
        before they hurt my beloveds.

But isn't it so that I sit safely on this hill
        where I assume righteousness
        yet only the brave step forward to brandish belief.

The Furies

Fumes of fire creep over the last ridge before pasture.
A great white sycamore shatters the oriole's net-nest.
River's autumn olive catches her fledgling, embraces its beating heart.
Singed by relentless summer, hills of hay waver/duck at the gale.

Flattened clay sweeps across ochre'd land once lush with grain.
A solitary Queen Anne's Lace leans listlessly an inch above the dirt.
From above, flashes of fierce heat aim at the yellow trucks.
Clang and sizzle linger as oiled flames lick the tires.

That's the western ridge, where they build relentlessly.
Here, the thin valley tapers into bosky poplar shadows.
Here, reprisal spills into trees scorned, fueled by rancor.
Backs to winged terror, giants bear wee babes. Fling them to safety.

Mother shivers, cradles the fevered child.
Pestilence as vengeance.
Man's callow disregard.
Their avarice. Their rapacity. Their nescience.

Heart of Sunflower

Out this window, cerulean sky, no clouds, not even the humble cirrus.
Splashes of emerald on sapphire
arms of poplar point plaintively
a female grosbeak intent on furtive pecks, on pace for Naples.

Pane smudged where old bear leaned into the bricks last night.
The shepherd jumped, cried, then curled into her covers.
A large window into this fleeting visit
punctuated by guilt and beauty.

Powdered iron slips over the mountain draught now.
Flattened streams of smoked ham reach toward the vale.
Dusky juncos pepper the chill grass, here till spring.
Will they miss me.

A Murmuration

A murmuration of gloss'd starlings sweeps in from southern foothills,
    defies a western wind, circles downward gleefully
        as turkey vultures hunch over their defeated prey, the king.

From the north runs a skulk of red fox toward the bloody field
    through dry leaves and sycamore balls and twigs
        left by scattered sparrows.

Men sought the king in silver winter, followed his kin, sent doe across
    the cold and rocky ridge. Never found him, the clever regent,
        who watched light leave their eyes beneath the low sky.

'Tis not wit nor skill that keeps me alive, the king told the forest,
    true, a certain wisdom brews with age
        but 'tis raw fortune that takes one and dispatches the other.

"If we are mark'd to die, we are enough," the bard had quoted Henry.
    A felled king on the valley floor breathed in the words
        as his tired hooves bent into frosted forage.

Ravens wait atop the pines. The red-tailed hawk rides biting thermals
    to clouds only to dive in waves
        toward the widening stain below.

When they were wee, the fox and the king skipped among dry leaves.
    Starlings and ravens watched a prince grow
        into an image, a mighty issue, of his own.

In January, light stretches across a red ridge toward the monastery.
    In January, red birds and black birds, bobcats and pasture mites
        test the teasing air.

In January, brothers die and sisters fall in cold embrace.
    Winter sits still among the dying.
    Spring will bury the blood.

The Great Dispersal

Kisses frantic in spring as the wood thrush awakens.
Breezes brush over cloud-scents of fresh clover. The red-tail squeals.
    How little we knew then, or cared, as sandpipers sprinted to shore.
Goldfinches swarm an old feeder I made, thinking it would last forever.

Courtship of swallows: golden breasts and proud ebony necks.
In late May, tunnels of sapphire plump beds of air for lustful larks.
    He built houses for bluebirds. Platforms for the jay.
Owls stir and join us for cocktails on the porch.

Frenzy of killdeer in the far south pasture. Flanking tadpoles in the marsh.
Meadowlarks sweep into greening grass. A kingbird reigns.
    They gather grasshoppers, crickets, ants, flies for mouths opened
    skyward.
June waltzes. In dark woods beyond the mossy hillock, we hear an oriole.

Suddenly, silence. I ask him what happened to the music of this airless night.
In July, he says, *their songs stop like that* (snap). Heat wafts from dry ground.
    They fly away soon and must rest. Take my hand, vanish as shadow.
I see now. A parched summer day pivots in haste from midday to the bitter dusk.

Ravens in the Wood

They warned the fair among us that our tans, rubbed with acorns, would turn
    would wrinkle
    would shock the mirror
    in time.

I dreamed of a girl like you. Airbrushed virgin olive, raven eyes, dark-lock corkscrews.
    Ojibwa and Celt
    dipped out of Doggerland
    you came.

Fierce, fire-some, relentless. A *kra* intense flashes down the mountainside.
    You soar.
    We embrace. Your fort, my paper.
    Alloy of feathers for the summit ahead.

Rufous Flies

Of a mind to garden
    on a sunny day
    old knees, fresh gloves

Late July with my straw hat
    tomatoes ripen
    johnny grass stifles the vines

As I struggle to weed, a stranger stops
    no one else in this weekday valley for miles around
    time out of order, the red-tail too young for almost-August

He's about six feet away, looks me square in the eye
    I rise. He jumps down, seems to limp, judges the next post
    and makes it four hands up

Is he hurt/his left wing offsides? Son says no, born late
    Next day at the garden the hawk waits. I name him.
    Every morn for a week we talk, in our way

Saturday, I hear his *heeeeeee*
    He's in the low willow by the spring
    then the maple then the ragged persimmon

Of a sudden, Rufous flies
    orange fan of a tail
    sights set on riverside sycamore one hundred yards hence

Another summer, a new straw hat
    Heeeee heeeeee he
    floats nearby, brings his bride. They call for the young

Last of the Blue Azures

Sit still. How many times I called out to that child. He had wings, and fins.
A whirly-gig of golden curls and mud-splattered shorts.
He chases his own child now.
He holds butterflies in a weathered hand and in her tender grace
      tiny fingers float just above the trembling life.

Are you a spring azure or a summer-spring azure?
There's a difference, did you know? Spring azure bubbles in clay at river's edge
stretches its inch. Tumbles alongside friends as the sun rolls north.
Cousin summer-spring rises at solstice and stays till frost.
      Lonesome mostly, a jumper, in soft country grass it skips righteously.

I save bugs now. The dog and I catch them in the kitchen at twilight,
Tupperware-top
flung among tall phlox. At this age, after these sorrows, I believe everyone
gets a last chance. Why shouldn't the garden spider return to its silk?
Why shouldn't a trembling amber dragonfly be freed into mountain's mist?
      Chance pulled me back. Evening lingers before the eyes of Jupiter.

Summer Spring

This year is rain.
Narrow, secreted mountain valley built of gneiss, quartz, clay.
The softest paths walked first before there were years.
Through a poplar-shaded pen, the seventh spring runs fast today.

Why do we do this? push people out of the way.
Who do we think we are? no different than they.

Rush of cold water through flattened sweet grass to the horse pasture. out east.
In the west, rushing stream so fast can't be pulled from the valley floor.
Between: no water. bad water. Lead and blue pistols.
Cold long hallways of keening.

What is green minted paper to a bear with her cubs?

The Ivy Tree

Years of sorrow round their shoulders, slivers of light poke sallow skin.
They touch beneath the ivy tree, years wrapped around a patient poplar,
hands entwined with knots and age
as the stubborn vine climbs.

Sorrows separated the keening years.
She buried the boy, raged, shattered flint.
He buried the boy, picked up
that she had strewn.

He built on a cleared mountain ridge. She swam in stinging salt water.

Rope braided by dappled light, leaves carefully folded into wax.
They both limp a bit now.
In each they see the river side of their youth.
Persimmon's bitterness sweeps aside.

What does the ivy tree see?

Branches reach one hundred feet high.
Ivy swallows the poplar tulip; in spring, they mate.
The Blackwater sends herons past, pushes warblers and kinglets
into the tangle.

Mockers wait amid lower vines, woodpeckers hammer wildly up high.
Behind ivy leaves, clinging to burnt bark, is the clarity of
transparent orbs left for summer
by buckeye butterflies.

Leave-Taking

Rushed ultramarine of the barn swallow, tawny fearsome
swift on the wing. So fast the horse can't see her but knows from falling straws
that she is building her raftered nest a third time this summer.

Three broods of lissome fledglings. They dare to sweep into the falling garden,
devour pesky gnats but only kiss the butterfly. Mother lines them up
along teetering umber planks above the roses below the cherry.

Garden walls waver with me. August wanes. A lane's walk downhill in
lonely wind.
Once, a girl dressed for school in plaid cotton, then shocked she felt the chill.
Sun sails southward toward nape of the valley. Dew challenges the western
heat.

Your babes flew at morning from an old garden to the willow. Today, you left.
We'd duck, quickly, when you chased us. Four hands running in a chuckle.
Only two palms now at the fall's edge, in solitary embrace of a spotted leaf.

Organelle

In miniature. Before sight. Banged out of rock.
Or faintly wallowing in steam,
this cell-piece clothed in translucent lipid
sent messengers to proteins that made you.

When west winds lift the spider's web, her silk floats in a soft line.
When a flying limb pierces the web, her drops roll as rivulets.
A message in me to you was pierced.
The boy a shimmering, brief illusion in tear-caked heat.

mRNA is the big hero now
yet the maskless push us up against walls,
scream their limp theories.
Multicellular giants glimpse back, clamber over graves unbelieving.

Umber dirt along the riverbank where we spread.
Anguish buried under johnny grass.

Papilio

Lemon-brushed, she has a final trip to make
across pastureland to the wild cherry tree.
Last meal on a frivolous zinnia, torn chiffon at her wings' end
amber and black turn to bisque on grey *appalachiensis*.

She shares the feast with me. I peer just beyond her proboscis
as gleefully she sips late summer's bounty.
Breeze tickles tired thinning locks
lifts her to the next flower.

At the wild cherry when steel circles sift vale-ward
she will place her last transparent orbs
and sleep.
Days pass as cracked acorns in swift cold wind. Dew's meadow fades.

The Talisman

Furnace fired brewed fried in a blast from the young sun scouring
the land, now soft and tame breathing lightly,
waiting for another thermal of flame.

Gneiss born from this, forced wildly and hot against crusts of diamond
falling flung fiercely
into shafts of flat land and onto angry mountains.

Gneiss - like face, like place, as in trace - huddles wearily atop calm hills here,
stones now grey and heavy as steel yet fetching reflected light
in crystal veins.

In this interlude, the cloudless sulphur swings silently
blindingly
a flirt of candy yellow against the solemn gneiss.

What have you done? the children cry.
Why?

Birds die, the river dries, spiked grass shoots blisters at our feet.
A sign, please. Conjure, fancy, cast cool hope in salty dew.
Like hillside stones afar, we shake. Question. Fear. We don't know how.

But the gneiss knows. Folly and chance will tempt a blaze.
Needles of quartz tumble through sky. Skirmishes light the valley below.
Stones shoot skyward, steaming.

Yet fevered beds again cool.
Rounded pastures green into blue.
Air crisp'd like brine then embraces sleep in cooling puffs.

Beside the cleaved gneiss
spit suddenly in ancient lightning
an amulet of quartz reflects.

Cloudless sulphur lifts in surprise
kisses striped stone
melts granite to gold.

Fibonacci's Flowers

In July's steaming sunlight, look closely at the rose.

Fibonacci knew roses, ambling along a stone wall in 1202

A century after the tower began to lean
his *Libra abaci* explained

The whirl of petals
one, one, two, three, five, eight, thirteen
a game

The golden ratio,
the gods' attempt at new math.
The nautilus, a snail
a hurricane, the galaxies
our fingers, and yours

Lily, sunflower, buttercup
nine hundred years once when he sat on a bench
facing Liguria
birdsong, azure skies, air like a crystal ball
dizzying rows to infinity
a cell precisely in threes fives eights
in circles predetermined
in silks woven one upon another in layers endless
Planning, precision whipped into cream

Burst chaos

Landing in neat order

If the gods could do this, if Fibonacci would tell us
why are we destroying the spirals now?

Marjorie Gowdy writes at home in the Blue Ridge mountains of Callaway, VA. Gowdy was Founding Executive Director of the Ohr-O'Keefe Museum of Art in Biloxi, MS, which she led for 18 years. Now retired, she worked in other fields that fed her love of writing, including as a grants writer.

Her poetry has been published in the *Roanoke Review* (2015), *Artemis Journal* (2013, 2018, 2019, 2020, 2021, 2022), *Floyd County Moonshine* (fall 2021 issue), *Valley Voices* (Mississippi Valley State University, in 2021), *Indolent Books* (online, January 2021), *Clinch River Review* 2021, *Visitant-Lit* (January 2021), *RockPaperPoem* (2022), the book *Quilted Poems* 2022, and art in the spring 2022 issue of *Orange Peel Magazine* and the 2021-22 *Gallerium: Extinction* catalog. Her essays are included in *Katrina: Mississippi Women Remember* (2007).

Gowdy also paints, with recent works accepted by the Virginia Beach Artists' Center (2020), illustrations published in *Floyd County Moonshine*, spring and fall 2021, in *Artemis Journal* 2021 (a visual poem), and included in an upcoming exhibition at the Virginia Tech *Carilion School of Medicine*. Her poems + verse, which she calls carmen duca, are also part of an exhibit, Welcome to Roanoke, in 2020-2021 at the Roanoke, VA, Municipal Building.

Gowdy is a summa cum laude graduate of Virginia Tech and has a master's degree in liberal studies from University of North Carolina-Greensboro. Her work is informed by the tumbled Virginia mountains as well as her time on the Mississippi Gulf Coast and along the coasts of Virginia and North Carolina. She is currently newsletter editor for the Poetry Society of Virginia.

www.ingramcontent.com/pod-product-compliance
Lightning Source LLC
Chambersburg PA
CBHW022129090426
42743CB00008B/1068